What People

⭐⭐⭐⭐⭐ **Inspirational!**

By Don J. Harper on August 12, 2015

Once I started reading this book I could not put it down (kindle). Very inspirational and motivating. As a teacher, I am always looking for innovative ways to reach the children. As a product of a low-income environment (poverty and other things...), I refused to allow those around me to bring me down. I love when I hear others repeat or spread the same message to those who want to listen. Great reading for people of all backgrounds.

⭐⭐⭐⭐⭐ **VULNERABLE MOTIVATION.**

ByTrekaon August 8, 2015

This was a refreshing and necessary book. I liked that this book was highly relatable, factual and blatantly honest. I respect the vulnerability and biblical references, it put a lot into perspective. This book motivated me to stay on my current path of lending my little bit of support to changing the world. This book isn't just for one group of people, it's just for the people. Everyone could take something from this. AMAZING WORK GABE!!! I can't wait for your next piece of inspiration. This world is in a state of emergency, this is the material warranted for recovery.

★★★★★ **Excellent Read!**

By E. Love on October 11, 2015

I really enjoyed this book and can't wait to continue the series! I love the way that Gabriel uses his own life experiences, biblical passages, and positive energy to make this a masterpiece that anyone can enjoy. I can't wait to read more from you Mr. Wallace. Great job!

★★★★★ **A great man, who has overcome**

By Reggie Harris on June 23, 2015

A great man, who has overcome! He has lived his writings! A man above men! This book will give you insights of overcoming not by someone who did research but was the results of his principles.

★★★★★ **Awesomely devised Body of Work from An Awesomely Devised Man of Integrity.**

By Adrian T. Ghent on July 11, 2015

Loved the transparency displayed throughout the Book of Revelations... I was so absorbed in the testimonies given. The Will of each story to strive for greater than their temporary circumstances was encouraging for me. Definitely a great read and a pivotal body of literature to add to anyone's personal library that is in search of absorbing words and steps towards inspiration.

★★★★★ **This book is awesome! It really details how you and God's grace...**

By Bobbie Nix on July 3, 2015

This book is awesome! It really details how you and God's grace control your life not your circumstances. Kudos to the author for being real. Can't wait for the next series.

The Journey

To

Better

10 Steps of Transforming

Poverty into Prosperity

The Transformation Series:

Phase 1-3

Gabriel Wallace

The Journey To Better

10 Steps of Transforming Poverty Into Prosperity

Copyright © 2017 Gabriel Wallace

DEDICATION

This book is dedicated to my Mom for her unconditional love, sacrifice and support.

TABLE OF CONTENTS

Phase 1: The Foundation

Phase 2: The Transition

Phase 3: The Growth Process

Acknowledgements

I wish to personally thank the following people for their contributions to my inspiration and knowledge and other help in creating this book: First off Praise be to the Most High God who always causes me to triumph. Dr. Craig Oliver, Dr. Letra Smith & My Elizabeth Baptist Church Family of Atlanta, GA. The John Maxwell Team. A special thanks to my family and friends for always believing in and supporting me throughout this entire process. Without your support, this would not be possible.

Foreword

Is your life everything you've ever dreamed of or is there something left to be desired? Do you even remember what it's like to dream? You know, when you were a kid and the responsibilities of day to day life hadn't kicked in yet. Everything seemed possible and there were no limits to what you could become. Well I am here to remind you that everything you dreamed was possible is possible regardless of your life experiences. I am a living witness that regardless of what path you take on this journey called life, you will always be capable of better.

Life will not always go as planned, but that's because you are not the planner, your Creator is. Your job is to cooperate with His plan for your life. The problem most of us have is that our plans and God's purpose do not align properly. Throughout this book, you will learn how you can align both and fulfill the life that you imagined while continuing the path that the Creator planned for you when you before you were born.

A dear friend of mine; I will refer to her as Stacy in order to respect her privacy, always wanted to be a professor at an Ivy League university. She didn't really like little kids, so she wanted to work on the college level. She knew exactly what she needed to do to accomplish her ambitious goals. Becoming pregnant, twice before graduating high school was in no way a part of her plan. But that didn't stop her. Sticking to her life goal, she decided not to go forward with her pregnancies. She went on to graduate high school with honors.

Once in college, Stacy's older sister died in a car accident which changed her life in more ways than one. She left behind two children that Stacy raised as her own. With her eye still on the prize, she finished college and enrolled in graduate school at the Ivy League university she intended to work for after she graduated.

In her junior year with everything on track she was now raising teenagers. One of her daughter's played soccer and ended up becoming best friends with a girl named Azel. Azel was of Ecuadorian descent and her parents came to the United States illegally. Before the start of the soccer season, Azel's parents went back to Ecuador in an attempt to get family into this country amidst the poverty, crime and drug problems that the country was facing. Azel's parents never returned from their trip. Stacy knew that Azel and her daughter were inseparable and Azel had no one in this country, so Stacy took her in. She couldn't stand to think about her being forced into the system. Azel was born in this country, therefore, a legal citizen so Stacy adopted Azel and raised her as her own. Stacy went on to graduate from college. It wasn't easy but she didn't let having three kids stop her. It wasn't easy but she did it.

After her graduation, she met a man named Tom who she later married. They raised the 3 children together as their very own. Stacy and her husband were happy with the 3 children and did not want any more. Then fate intervened; Stacy became pregnant. Still carrying the painful memories of her high school experience, she decided to see this pregnancy through. She had just received a job at the Ivy League she'd dreamed about, but not as a professor. She wasn't worried about it because she just knew she would eventually get there.

When Stacy's waters broke, she had no idea what would happen next. The sonographer somehow missed one important piece of information. Stacy wasn't pregnant with one, but two babies. She gave birth to a pair of healthy twins.

Stacy ended up getting a job at a local university but never became an Ivy League College professor. She never imaged having 5 children; 3 of them not of her own and two unplanned. Stacy's plan and God's purpose were not the same as Stacy never wanted children. But God had her life planned before she was created. Stacy would have said you were crazy if you told her what her life would be when she started college. Her journey came with a lot of pain, heartache, death and every other tragedy imaginable. Stacy had a basic plan but God had something better. Once Stacy allowed life to guide her journey; never giving up and doing what she felt was right, she positioned herself on the path to her destiny. Throughout this book, you will learn to use the obstacles in your life as simple road signs to guide on your journey to better.

Preface

The Iraq war veteran Kevin Powers wrote, "As human beings, we have the blessing and the curse that we're able to adapt to almost anything. No matter how extreme the circumstances you're in, they become normal."

This statement is true on so many distinct levels. In many cases, our circumstances become our reality. Unfortunately, adverse conditions breed negativity, limit expectations and paralyze growth. Our past experiences are the frame of reference for our future. We carry around so much emotional baggage from our past that it weighs us down and eventually we give up and accept mediocrity. In other words, we give up on being more and doing more than the limits set by our society. At some point in time, in life, everybody has dreamed of being a superhero or a person of great significance, but over time we have allowed life's trials and tribulations to overshadow our aspirations.

The book that you have before you started about 10 years ago to serve as a release or therapeutic mechanism for past emotional wounds that needed to be disinfected, stitched up and healed. Especially the wounds of unforgiveness, which will destroy you from the inside out if not reconciled. That quickly changed with the realization that there are so many people, young and old, fighting strongholds and losing the battle going through life lost with no clue why they are feeling these different emotions and frustrations. After years of soul searching, trial and error, and, finally, divine wisdom, I am convinced that God has revealed the steps to transform a mindset of poverty into one of prosperity and triumph. These steps have allowed me to turn "My Scars into Stars". By God's grace and mercy, I was spared in order to lead generations to come.

Everything that I experienced was a part of a divine purpose to know the way and show the way to people across the world. John Maxwell, leadership expert and author, said this: "Anyone can steer the ship, but it takes a leader to chart the course."

I was born and raised in Greenwood, Mississippi. Greenwood is in the Mississippi Delta Region, "The Armpit of the state of Mississippi", and continues to reflect systematic and long-term economic depression that stifles the quality of life for many of its inhabitants. Greenwood possesses stagnant growth, a low high school graduation rate (compared to the nation) and a poverty rate that is much higher than the national average. The Mississippi Delta is known for being the birthplace of the blues and good ol' home cooking. On the flip side, it has a deep, dark history dating from the Civil War and the Civil Rights Movement that left scars that continue to affect generations. Mississippi ranks dead last economically. The Delta region is one of poorest regions in the US. The Delta illustrates the huge income disparity. The region is one of the most economically and educationally deprived areas in the country. More than 30 million children are growing up in poverty. In 2011, nearly 46.2 million Americans were living in poverty.

Children living in poverty have a higher number of absenteeism or leave school altogether because they are more likely to have to work and care for family members.

16 to 24-year-old students who come from low-income families are seven times more likely to drop out than those from families with higher incomes. Only about 62% of adults in the Mississippi Delta have a high school diploma compared to 80% nationwide. Adults in Mississippi have the highest rate of illiteracy in the nation, with 30% scoring as Level 1, which basically is less than fifth-grade level reading and comprehension skills. A higher percentage of young adults (31%) without a high school diploma live in poverty, compared to the 24% of young people who finished high school. 40% of children living in poverty aren't prepared for primary schooling. Children who live below the poverty line are 1.3 times more likely to have developmental delays or learning disabilities than those who don't live in poverty.

By the end of the 4th grade, African-American, Hispanic and low-income students are already 2 years behind grade level. By the time, they reach the 12th grade they are four years behind. The nation's lowest-performing high schools produce 58% of all African-American dropouts and 50% of all Hispanic dropouts, compared to 22% of all white dropouts. Less than 30% of students in the bottom quarter of incomes enroll in a 4-year school. Of that group, less than 50% graduate.

Mississippi also leads the nation in its number of health care problems. It has the highest rate of heart disease and the second highest rate of diabetes in the country. ABC news reported that five U.S. counties with the lowest life expectancies for women are in the Mississippi Delta region. The life expectancy is lower than nations of Honduras, Peru or El Salvador. These staggering findings can be compared to just about any urban community across the nation. These social and economic disparities adversely impact the mental conditions of those who live in these environments.

Someone who is looking from the outside in might say, "It's not my problem." I beg to differ. Either directly or indirectly, it affects everyone in some shape, form or fashion. Make the pledge to join the struggle and be a part of the solution, not the problem. We can't sit back any longer and merely hold on to what we have and not reach back to help the less fortunate.

This is not about giving money. It's going to take time, effort, and unlimited resources to right the wrongs of this systematic oppression. Most are born in these conditions and, in turn, are molded to think and act certain ways based on their reality. Rather than judge or turn our backs, let's be the people who God created us to be—the kind of people who love unconditionally and will sacrifice self to help another in need.

The Bible states in the book of Mark 12:31 (NIV) *The second is this: 'Love your neighbor as yourself'.* There is no commandment greater than these. We should always treat others the way we would like to be treated. If we take this approach we can help advance those from less favorable conditions to rise above their current circumstances by giving them options that they didn't know existed.

Everyone will have their fair share of setbacks. Some more than others. Some worse than others. Some will be self-inflicted while some are from past transgressions of generations that came before us. The Bible states in *Matthew 5:45 (KJV) ...for he maketh his sun to rise on the evil and on the good, and sendeth rain on the just and on the unjust.*

The upside of this is that He won't put more on us that we can bear. So, fret not, good and faithful servant, because he will never leave you nor forsake you. Psalm 23 1:6 (KJV) has always given me peace in the eye of the storm. It reads:

1 The LORD is my shepherd; I shall not want.

2 He maketh me to lie down in green pastures: he leadeth me beside the still waters.

3 He restoreth my soul: he leadeth me in the paths of righteousness for his name's sake.

4 Yea, though I walk through the valley of the shadow of death, I will fear no evil: for thou art with me; thy rod and thy staff they comfort me.

5 Thou preparest a table before me in the presence of mine enemies: thou anointest my head with oil; my cup runneth over.

6 Surely goodness and mercy shall follow me all the days of my life: and I will dwell in the house of the LORD forever.

This book is about learning to forgive your past and enlarging your vision for the future God has planned for your life. You might be feeling sorry for yourself, down on your luck with a defeated mentality and ready to throw a pity party about how terrible your life is. This isn't fair you might say to yourself. Maybe you are right. In the meantime, you must do the best you can with what you have. We can't control who our parents are or where we were born, but we can control our attitude. Your thoughts control your life. Henry Ford stated, "Whether you think you can or you think you can't – you're right." Always be able to find a positive in every negative. Decide to be the victor and not the victim. You will need a lot of help on your journey to better. So, build a solid foundation with God's Word and develop a personal relationship with the Creator through Jesus Christ. Your faith will be what sees you through. In order for you to exercise your faith, you must know what the Word says. In Ephesians 6:11-13 (KJV) it reads Put on the whole armor of God, that ye may be able to stand against the strategies of the devil. 12 For we wrestle not against flesh and blood, but against principalities, against powers, against the rulers of the darkness of this world, against spiritual wickedness in high places. 13 Therefore, put on every piece of God's armor so you will be able to resist the enemy in the time of evil. Stand firm. God will see you through. If he brings us to it he will bring us through it. Always recognize and give glory unto God who always causes us to triumph.

The Journey To Better

10 Steps of Transforming Poverty into Prosperity

The Transformation Series:

Phase 1 - The Foundation

Introduction

I was born to a single mother of six. I am the youngest of all my siblings. My earliest memories as a child are watching my father beat my mother to bloody pulps at times. For over ten straight years, we traveled for miles down long roads of only catfish ponds and cotton fields to visit my father in prison. The trip there felt like it took forever, but the trip back was always worse. My mother traveled those long roads back bloody, swollen and in silence.

My childhood was packed with vivid memories of horrific events that played out in front of me. I was around 4 years old when my father went to prison, yet I remember him holding a gun to one of my brothers' head, holding him as a hostage while in a shootout with my grandfather. My environment was a bottomless pit of negativity and damnation. From selling drugs to gang banging was a way of life.

All I knew was what I saw. By the age of sixteen, I had been arrested at least three times. My dad spent most of his years in prison and eventually died there. Two of my older brothers were lost in the streets. These were my role models and the only male figures I had in my life.

There was a vicious generational curse running through my bloodline that I was predisposed to. It controlled and distorted my view on life. Eventually, through the favor, grace, and mercy of God, I was able to overcome my circumstances.

My transformation started in a moment. One day my mother found drugs and money underneath my bed. She looked at me with tears in her eyes. It was the first time I ever saw her cry. It broke my heart to see the pain I caused her because she sacrificed everything to raise us right. Every day she walked for miles to work the three jobs she had to support our family. After I admitted to the drugs she told me that I was her last hope for the family and that it was up to me to break the vicious cycle soliciting me as its next victim. Her words weighed heavily on my heart. It was truly a life-changing moment.

For the first time ever, I felt a sense of purpose. I wanted nothing more than to break our destructive cycle and eventually I did. I was the first and the youngest in my family to graduate from college. Since then my oldest brother has changed his life around and finished his degree. One of my sisters finished her degree and another finished her associates as well. Another one of my brothers is enjoying his career as a fireman. In 2000, I signed a full athletic scholarship to attend Mississippi State University to play football. I became the light and joy of my family and community. My journey continues.

I decided to answer the calling on my life, so I changed careers to put myself in a position to serve others and help them reach their full potential. I had known the calling on my life for quite some time, but I was so engulfed in my career I just continued to put it on the backburner.

The moment that you know God's purpose for your life and what the scripture entails, you are accountable. It's just a matter of time before God closes doors or allows things to happen to get your attention for you to be in line with your assignment. I will be honest; one day, in church, I found out that God holds us accountable per everything we know in the Word. I immediately stopped listening to the sermon, closed my Bible, and considered taking a break from going to church for a while. I looked around as if God was sitting all around me. I laughed, shook my head, and said to myself that the devil is a liar.

In this book, I will show you how he is a liar. More than that, I will show you how to reach the purpose that God set forth for you before you were born.

You do not need to know the Bible or attend church every Sunday to benefit from this book. All you need is an open heart, mind, and little bit of faith. I can assure you that if you apply these steps into your everyday life, you will get positive results. This is your moment. I celebrate you as you begin your journey to better.

Step 1

Determine the Enemy

Jer 29:11

For I know the plans I have for you," declares the Lord,"

plans to prosper you and not to harm you, plans to give you

Hope and a future.

God's word says there are great plans on God's agenda for you. God wants you to prosper and increase on all sides. He wants you to break forth to the right, left and center. There is no plan of poverty or sickness in His plan for you.

Have you ever wondered why the devil is trying so hard to make you miserable and all your effort futile?

The reason is not far-fetched from this great plan of God for you. It is why the devil is working so hard. He knows that quite a few of us are not aware of our privileges in God. He then uses our ignorance to our disadvantage.

1 Peter 5:8 reads, "be alert and of sober mind. Your enemy the devil prowls around like a roaring lion looking for someone to devour"

Have you ever wondered what it would be like to be in a fight blindfolded? It's just like shadow boxing or playing "Hit the Piñata"; exactly what some of us are doing against an adversary strong enough to make a shipwreck of nations?

An adversary is a person, group, or force that opposes or attacks, often referred to as an enemy. You are up against a real enemy and he wants to get you as far away from your purpose as possible.

Note: An adversary does not stand against you failing, but rather against you succeeding!

To defeat or overcome the enemy, you must know who it is and what it wants. Most people growing up within poor urban communities would suggest that the enemy is our set of adverse circumstances or social conditioning. It will surprise you to know that you are most times the one to take responsibility for the way things have turned out to be in your life. Although the outer conditions of a person's life shape their reality, it is still ultimately your choices that determine success or failure. "You are Braver than you believe, stronger than you seem, and smarter than you think," -Christopher Robbins from Winnie the Pooh

Through my eyes, there were no options, only traditions, which I later found out to be generational curses. These are spiritual bondages or strongholds that are passed down from one generation to another. Satan is aware of these issues and really lures you in by suggesting negative things to partake in.

Ignorance, your great enemy.

Imagine you are in a serious financial mess because you haven't been able to pay your rent. You ran to someone who happens to be my friend. During your discussion, I overheard and decided to help without your knowledge. Do you know if I go ahead to pay our rent, your house owner can still go ahead to harass you because you don't know what has been done for you until knowledge of what I have done comes to know?

This is exactly the case of many people. Christ has paid for all you owed and has supplied for all you need. Do you know that? You may be asking yourself "if that is the case, then why am I still poor and devastated?" That is exactly what I'm sharing with you.

Let's consider God's word.

Gal 3:13: "Christ redeemed us from the curse of the law by becoming a curse for us, for it is written:

Cursed is everyone who is hung on a tree."

Verse 14 He redeemed us in order that the blessing given to Abraham might come to the Gentiles through Christ Jesus so that by faith we might receive the promise of the Spirit.

It is for a purpose that Christ died. He did not just pay off your rent to leave you in a terrible state whereby living from hand to mouth. He also deposited some goodies in your account that can carry you for the rest of your life. Yes, I mean for the rest of your life.

Notice the scripture says in verse 14 that the purpose is for us to be blessed. Rid yourself of ignorance.

Guard your mind

Proverbs 4:23; Keep your heart with all diligence, for out of it spring the issues of life.

Why do you think the scriptures will admonish to guard your heart? It is natural that you play a tune with your mind though you never listened to it intentionally. What the music was playing was entering your heart unconsciously.

The issues of life are as this. Many negative words come into and upon your life. So many brings you into an awareness of what you cannot do. It is thus natural for you to think impossibility and failure when all you hear is negative and impossibilities. That is the reason why you are responsible for your present situation. God is not the one making you suffer neither is it that any human has a direct control over your life. If anything happens, you permitted it.

I really was on the road of destruction. I once choked a guy until he passed out and beat him up over $4 dollars. In a more serious infraction, I broke a huge tree branch over the face of a guy who owed me money for drugs. The victim had to be admitted to ICU. There are far too many situations for me to name them all. It's important to know how the devil will use your mind as a playground if you let him. Before I was freed from the curse, by accepting Jesus Christ as my Lord and savior, the enemy constantly reminded me of my bloodline. He planted negative seeds of how my father was a drug dealer, murderer, and a menace to society. He wanted me to accept that as my fate. My father warned me about this. He told me the only way to overcome it was to turn my life over to God.

There was a story I read about a pregnant dog that was hit by a car and her back legs were severely damaged, which caused her to drag them. The puppies were soon born and began to drag their legs the same way. The owner was confused so he took them to the vet to see if they'd suffered any injuries. It turned out that the puppies were perfectly fine. Turns out that they were just going by what they saw modeled. Does that sound familiar to anyone? You see, we are socially conditioned by what we see. Before I was baptized I was tortured by nightmares of violent rage and unrest. This goes far beyond learned behavior. See, the devil enters through the gateway of the flesh, which is referred to as our sinful nature. To close the door to our flesh, we must first be filled with the Word of God and the Holy Spirit that lives within us. Secondly, we must be able to pick up our cross daily and follow Him. The good news is that generational curses can be broken. I am a living testimony.

As a child, I was subjected to so many negative, destructive, and paralyzing conditions that it plagued my soul. I saw so many horrible things that I suppressed them and eventually became desensitized. I remember the first time I witnessed a murder. My friends and I were just hanging out when we heard a loud gunshot close by. We ran to see what happened. Upon arrival, we saw the killer walk away into the alley while the victim lay stiff dead with a bullet in his head. It took the ambulance and local authorities an hour to make it to the scene of the crime. In that instant, there were two things that bothered me. 1. Watching the brains of the victim just fall out of his head when the paramedics picked him up. 2. The cry of a father. (The victim's father arrived on the scene and totally broke down to his knees, crying out, "LET ME SEE MY SON!") Unfortunately, he was already wrapped in plastic. From that point on my reality was formed. The tragic part about the situation is that the victim came from a well-to-do family, so he had a choice but chose unwisely and paid the ultimate price of losing his life.

It took me 27 years to escape that reality. I finally felt freedom from my past and could now embrace my future. You see, I had acquired false beliefs from the conditional entrapment of my circumstances. They controlled my thoughts, influenced my behaviors and dictated my choices. Your self-image can either propel or derail your future. So, I ask again, who is the enemy? There will be so many things that happen to you in life that are beyond your control. What you do have control of is your response. Remember this statement: Events plus reaction equals outcome. The war within yourself is between good and evil. Whichever one you feed the most will win. Now that your true enemy has been revealed, be brave and refuse to be held captive by your environment. Make sure that you are constantly evaluating your patterns of behavior and filling your spirit with positive images to ensure that you are governed accordingly. You either create your environment or it creates you. Be diligent in finding your own truth. For the truth is the light and the light will set you free.

Action point: *Be informed of your privileges in God and rid yourself of people that speak negatives words over your life. And those that show you your weakness and impossibilities*

Step 2

Look Outside Yourself

Have you ever struggled with any issues in your life that you could not seem to control or shake off? What did you do to change the situation or create a different result? Or did you just get frustrated and give up? Many of us try to power through and hopefully come out better on the other side. Before I knew better that was my answer, my cure-all. When all else fails, continue to push through and never give up. This usually works temporarily; however, deeper issues will usually come back with a vengeance when you're at your weakest moments in life. We begin to search high and low for answers when they are right in front of our face. It is hard to see the picture when you are in the frame.

What you need to know in these moments is that you have access to a greater power; the power of God that residents in the person of the Holy Spirit. The Holy Spirit is the one that makes available the power of God to us and in us. The Holy Spirit is the gift of God for believers. When the Holy Spirit is upon your life, anything is possible.

The Lord Jesus Christ couldn't do anything until he was anointed with the Holy Spirit. Scriptures record that when Jesus was being baptized by John the Baptist, "the heavens opened and the Holy Spirit came upon Him." He needed the power of the Holy Spirit to fulfill his God-given purpose. Notice when He was to leave the earth, He told the disciples to wait in Jerusalem until they are endued with power from on high. We all need this same power from on high.

This was the power that emboldened the Apostles. Until the Holy Spirit came on them, they were just ordinary fishermen and physician. But when the power on high came on them, they became different people. The same possibilities are available to you. When you have the power of the Holy Spirit in you, you become different; powerful. Everything that once seemed impossible becomes possible. No power can stand against you.

Think about some of your toughest struggles. Take a few minutes to write down a couple of them. Think about some of your family members. Do you see similar patterns of behavior? If you're not sure ask questions. You may need to do some research. Start by talking with a couple of elders in the family, friends of family or even long-standing members of a church or organization your family has been associated with. I can guarantee that you were not the first in your family to deal with the issues you are facing. The good news is that you can be the first to change them. You have a choice. Continue to fight a losing battle or release it to a higher power other than yourself. Lean not on your own understanding and you are limited. Lean on God to win. The Book of Ephesians reminds us that He is not limited by lack of imagination, creativity, vision or power as we are. Therefore, cast your cares and burdens upon God and He will give you peace.

In life, there will be trials and tribulations that make you want to question your faith but God will remain faithful and just. That is why the Holy Spirit functions as our comforter. You need to know that it is Gods will for you to prosper and be in good health. The Holy Spirit brings you into remembrance of God's promises to you. Sometimes He has to take you through, to get you to a point where He can utilize the gifts He has equipped you with. A great teammate and friend of mine from high school, by the name of Michael Archie, experienced a tragic and unthinkable life-altering event in the fall of 2003. Let me rewind back a couple of years first to paint the picture of what and who Mike was prior to this event. Mike was a multi-sport athlete and a scholar. His passion and claim to fame was basketball. My senior year, his junior in high school, we managed to go undefeated during the regular basketball season and made it to the semi-finals of the state tournament. Our overall record was 31-4 finishing at the #6 team in the state. He garnered numerous awards and accolades throughout his prominent career, the most notable being named 2001 Dandy Dozen, 2001 Commonwealth Player of the Year, and 2001 McDonald All-American nominee. He was also selected to compete in the 2001 MS/ALA All-Star game.

After high school, Michael went to college to compete on a different level and boy did he. Freshmen year he averaged 12 points and 6 rebounds per game. His sophomore season started out promising, averaging around 17 points per game. He was living a dream and destined for a promising career until tragedy struck. On Saturday January 26, 2003, following a victory over a rival opponent, Mike, and a few teammates decided to celebrate the win at a local nightclub. A fight erupted inside the club, gunshots rang out and he was struck by a stray bullet, leaving him paralyzed from the waist down. His life was changed forever.

Sweet dreams quickly turned into a nightmare. This really hit home for me. I was in a state of shock and disbelief. Years passed by and I finally asked the question, "What was it like and how did you recover from that major setback?" He replied, "As I look back on my life and the trials that I've overcome, I truly believe that there has been a divine presence with me every step of the way. I made it only by the grace of God, a lot of prayers and support. Sure, my competitive nature helped push me to do what I needed to do, and the fact that my family didn't expect any less of me was motivation. But you don't make it through what I've had to endure without a higher power working in your favor. We, as humans, make plans for our lives and certain goals we want to have accomplished by a certain age.

What we fail to realize is that God has a plan for your life as well. My plan was to play professional basketball and make a lot of money. God's plan for me was different. To this day, I have yet to ask God, 'Why did you let this happen to me?' Only that He used me according to his divine plan. It is my faith that allows me to focus on the positive and continue to strive for greatness. It could've been a lot worse. I could've been dead 12 years ago. That is why I appreciate and live each day to its fullest. We, as humans, all have trials and tribulations that we must endure. These trials come in different situations so there's really no comparison. We all have the choice to succumb or overcome. I made my choice 12 years ago, and I haven't looked back. You don't really know how strong you are until you have to show it. As for me, I can do all things through Christ who strengthens me."

There is always a choice. No one would have blamed Mike if he just disappeared off the face of the earth. Despite all the obstacles life threw his way he chose to live rather than exist. Now Mike is married and still has a sweet jump shot. Yes, this was a tragic event that changed the course of his life, but an even greater tragedy would have been if he didn't learn and grow from his experience. Mike allowed this set back to push him into his divine purpose in life. When you choose to walk in faith you possess the same power that raised Christ from the dead. It is our faith that allows us to tap into the power of the Holy Spirit. Which will you magnify, your problem or your GOD? Always keep hope alive. Remember, no matter what you are going through, no weapon formed against you shall prosper.

Action point: The power of God is resident in the person of the Holy Spirit. Seek to have the Holy Spirit in you and the power of God will rest mightily in you. Shalom

Step 3

Face Your Truth

Do you want the truth about the journey ahead or would you prefer me to comfort you by telling you everything will be ok and things will just work themselves out through osmosis? So, which do you choose? "You Can't Handle The Truth!" The facts state the chances of you going to prison are greater than you going to college. In 16 states, there are more people in prisons and jails than college housing. The facts state 1 out of 3 girls and 1 out of 5 boys will be sexually abused before they reach the age of 18.

Research tells us that within the poor inner-city areas there will be very limited healthcare available, living conditions will be at or below the poverty level, and there will be limited access to gainful employment. Wait a minute, there is more. Recently, further research has been conducted linking inner city children to post-traumatic stress disorder (PTSD). "Youth living in inner cities show a higher prevalence of post-traumatic stress disorder than soldiers," per Howard Spivak M.D., director of the U.S. Centers for Disease Control and Prevention's Division of Violence Prevention.

These factors have adverse impacts on getting a quality education. Teachers face insurmountable challenges to provide an environment conducive for learning, while parents can't or won't invest the time to prepare their children for school. Some are busy working 2-3 jobs while others have their priorities mixed up. "Some teachers may interpret students' emotional and social deficits as a lack of respect or manners, however, the reality is that students come to school with a narrower range of appropriate emotional responses than we expect."

The truth is that many children simply don't have the repertoire of necessary responses. It is as though their brains' "emotional keyboards" play only a few notes." This truth is hard to swallow. It's like drinking razor blades. First off, you don't necessarily see or feel the adverse effects of the circumstances. But when we slow down and examine our mental state the deep cuts and wounds have disintegrated any hope for the future. "What did I do to deserve this?" you may ask. Maybe I am just having a bad dream, so let me close my eyes, click my heels and repeat, "There's no place like home," 3 times and my problems will go away. Dorothy from the Wizard of Oz was on to something.

There will be times when you will need to depend on your imagination to get you through, however, you must face the brutal truth about your current set of circumstances.

One of my best friends, named Mario, moved to Mississippi in middle school. I think it was the sixth grade if I remember correctly. He was an outsider and we all know how foreigners are welcomed with open arms, right? His first experience of southern hospitality was a crack to the jaw. Every day Mario had to fight for respect. He could not enjoy attending any afterschool functions without acknowledging the fact that he might be jumped or chased all the way home. Boy, could he run. He persevered through it all with a positive attitude.

Mario was determined not to live in fear and chose to enjoy life. He eventually gained respect mostly due to his ability to perform on the basketball court. Wherever there was a basketball court he would play and compete against whomever, no matter the environment. That same tenacity helped our high school basketball team to a 28-0 record during the regular season and ranked number 2 in the state. It would have been easy for him to just disappear and stay cooped up in the house, but he chose to live outside of his comfort zone.

You can't control where you were born, but you can control your attitude regarding the situation. Life is less about what happens to us and more about how we respond to the challenges we face. In the game of life, you cannot simply press the reset button when things fall apart. At times, your body will feel fully submerged in trials and tribulations, making it hard to breathe. The deck is stacked against you. Look at the bright side. When the smoke clears, you are still standing. That means that your life still has a purpose to fulfill. The way I see it is if I am breathing, everything else is extra credit. God is still with you. He will never leave you nor forsake you. The Bible reads, in Psalms 92:12, the righteous will flourish like palm trees. A palm tree is resilient. They are usually the only thing standing after a hurricane. They may bend to the point where they touch the ground, but they don't break. The roots are very flexible and grow stronger after going through adverse conditions of a hurricane or tropical storm. We are no different. Therefore, you must choose to magnify your God and not your problems.

In the movie 300, a Persian warlord says to a Spartan, "A thousand nations of the Persian empire will descend upon you. Our arrows will blot out the sun!" The Spartan replies, with a smirk on his face, "Then we will fight in the shade." That battle really depicts the challenge that lies ahead for you. The Spartans were able to stand firm against an enemy that outnumbered them by the tens of thousands. "How?" They had a plan and they were prepared both physically and mentally. You were built to adapt and overcome any situation. To conquer your enemy, you must live in the Word, be filled with the Holy Spirit, and equipped with fellow believers to aid and support you in battle. We are often blindsided by issues and are forced to react, leaving us falling further behind. From there we fall into a rut and that rut turns into a grave.

My good friend Chris shared his testimony about how God has given him hope and peace from a dark and tragic beginning. "At the age of 5 I remember my mother dating this guy for about 6 months. Those 6 months changed my life forever. I could tell she feared something, but I didn't know what it was. My mother's boyfriend really wasn't that great of a person. I could tell something seemed off about him. He would do horrible things in front of my siblings and me. I remember some of the things he did to me, from watching porn in front of me to letting his dog jump on my siblings and I so we did whatever he said to do. He cussed us out as if we were grown-ups. I was too scared to tell my mother about those things.

I remember one day my mom was teaching me how to use the phone. The only number she taught me was 911. She told me if something bad ever happened to dial 911. A few days had gone by; I was playing with my 3-month-old baby brother when tragedy struck the family. My mom was with her friends getting their hair done in the kitchen. The front door suddenly flew open. It was my mom's boyfriend with a gun. I was frozen with fear. He walked right past me as if I wasn't there. I watched him shoot one of my mom's friends, who was sitting closest to the refrigerator, first. Then he turned to her other friend who was pregnant at the time. After that he grabbed my mom by the hair and dragged her across the floor then threw her into the room and closed the door. When he closed the door, I grabbed my baby brother and went to hide in the closet. I was terrified. All I heard was yelling, screaming and a few more gunshots. I opened the door to see if he had left. The next thing I saw was unthinkable. After being shot, my mom was crawling on the floor when he grabbed her by her hair and shot her one last time. He then sprinted out the house, jumped in his truck and drove off. I finally walked out of the closest and just started crying. The first body I saw was my mom's. I just stared hopelessly while standing in her blood. After seeing this, I walked into the kitchen and collapsed from shock. I just remember crying at the top of my lungs. At the age of 5 I could not digest or understand what happened. All I knew or felt was loneliness.

After the smoke cleared my 4 siblings and I were separated into different foster homes. I thought that I would never see them again. Through the grace of God, my grandparents adopted and reunited us. This gave me hope. On the way to the funeral with my grandparents I remember asking where my mother was going. They told me that I would see her in heaven. I then asked them, "Where is heaven?" They told me, "In the sky." I just looked up at the sky the whole time on the way to and from the funeral. Twenty-one years later I still have questions about who I am, what I am, and why was I spared. I am far from where I want to be in my relationship with God, but I know that He has me in the palm of His hands. It is only God who gives me the strength to persevere and remain positive through it all."

God never promised us that this life would be easy, however He did promise to pay back those who believe double for their trouble. Think about the story of Job. Think about his unwavering faith and how he was restored by God. Job 42:10 reads, When Job prayed for his friends, the Lord restored his fortunes. In fact, the Lord gave him twice as much as before. So now that you know better you should do better. You can start by praising and thanking God instead of complaining about how terrible things are. Complaining only cuts off the blessings God has in store for you. Once you start to honor and acknowledge how good God is, the angels go to work on your behalf. After all, if life was easy there would be no need for faith. God allows us to go through things to build our character to carry out a divine purpose. We always grow and develop in dark places; just like a seed that is planted in the dirt, the roots grow strong first before you see anything blossom. Declare now that, no matter what life throws your way, you will bless the Lord at all times. Give yourself away and allow him to work through you. Get out of the way and take the limits off God. Seek first the kingdom above all else and everything you need will be provided.

This brings us to a close of Phase 1 **The Foundation**. Now that you have something to build upon take some time to yourself to digest and process it all. As you apply the steps keep in mind that Rome was not built in a day. I look forward to continuing our journey into Phase 2 **The Transition**

Action point: *Be courageous enough to face the truth no matter how difficult it seems. The interesting thing is, truth will always set you free.*

The Journey

To Better

10 Steps of Transforming Poverty into Prosperity

The Transformation Series:

Phase 2 - The Transition

Introduction

Success is defined as the achievement of goals, but Luke 12:15 paints a bigger picture of success; the achievement of God's goals for your life. Success is not what you do or what you acquire. Success is who you are. When you achieve the goals God has set for your life, He considers you a success. The Lord told Jeremiah that "I knew you before I formed you in your mother's womb. Before you were born I set you apart and appointed you as my prophet to the nations." (**Jer 1:5, Jer10:23; Jer 29:11**). You were created a success.

Transformation can be said to be the mother of success. It reconnects you to the true essence of who you are and the intentions set for your life. Without transformation, success seems unattainable. The sole purpose of transformation is to **GROW IN** so you can **GROW OUT**. The person you are inside will determine the person you become on the outside. Once the necessary changes take place within you, you will be able to fulfill your purpose.

Whatever you believe in your heart it what you will be? Do you believe that you are a success? The heart of the matter is a matter of the heart, so once you get success in your heart you have no other choice than to act it out. Therefore, to grow in life and ministry, we must first **GROW IN**, because success flows from the heart (**Prov. 23:7; Prov. 27:17; Prov. 4:23; Matt. 12:25 (amp.); III John 2**). You don't see people, things and situations in life the way they are, you see them the way you are. (**I John 4:4, 5:4**) Who you are determines what you see.

Step 4

Find a Mentor

Jeremiah 3:15

"And I will give you shepherds after my own heart, who will guide you with knowledge and understanding."

A mentor is a person with experience who advises and guides someone with less experience over a period of time. Basically, a mentor does not necessarily have to be where you are going but he must be along the path you are going and, he must be way ahead of you. The bible says: "the less is blessed of the better." For anyone to be a blessing to you in mentorship, he must be better than you.

Having established a foundation for transition in your life, it is imperative that you have a mentor to guide you through. Prov. 11:14 says "Where no counsel is, the people fall: but in the multitude of counselors there is safety." Transformation is not a painless process. Having someone to help lift you up through the process will but guarantee a successful transition.

There are two things that you may want to consider when it comes to obtaining and maintaining a mentor. They are attractability and teachability.

Let's start with attractability. Webster defines attractability as the quality or fact of being attractable. You don't just want anyone mentoring you; you want the person who God has assigned to bless your life. God's favor will position you to be in the right place for the right person to be attracted to you. But, to receive this favor, you must submit to the will of God and do your part from an appearance and behavioral standpoint. You can and will miss out on your blessings if you fail to allow God's light to shine through you.

One day after school, on my way to football practice, a lady was unloading the marching band equipment from her vehicle. Being the gentlemen that I am, I stopped what I was doing and asked if she needed assistance. She smiled and said "I sure would. We need more young men like you." I helped her unload and before I would walk away she gave me money, and looked me in eyes with empathy as she told me of how she knew my mom and our challenging family situation. She also said if I ever needed anything, I should give her a call. From that day on our relationship grew. She welcomed me into to her family as a son. I consider her as my true appointed God mother.

Her guidance and love has enriched my life more than she will ever know. She gave me hope for a better future. For that reason, I am forever indebted. Her name is Mrs. Cheron Baines. God aligned our paths. This was an example of loving thy neighbor so God showed me favor for doing his will. Your deeds are seeds for a future harvest. You shall reap what you sow.

Secondly, you must be teachable. While attractability will lead a mentor to you, teachability allows for the relationship to flourish. It's what lets your mentor know that you are committed to the process, which makes he or she want to remain committed to you. To maintain a mentor, you must humble yourself and allow him or her to pour into you. You must give them permission to lead you. I was blessed to have several mentors throughout my journey. Some of what I learned had an immediate impact while other things happened later in my transition and maturation process.

Mentors come in many different forms. They could be a neighbor, a member of your church, or in my case, an athletic coach. When you're young, a coach's words can carry more weight than your parents or teachers. For me, my coaches' words were like that of a parent. I viewed them as father figures, which filled a void in my life.

I had a few coaches but the first coach that made an impact in my life was Mr. Larry "Kite" Johnson. Kite was one of the basketball coaches and owner of a local recreation center. The recreation center helped raise so many young men. While playing for Kite I learned the art of discipline and respect. Kite had a couple of strong arm tactics that would be considered child abuse nowadays. The infamous pinch was his signature. If you were non-compliant, he would grab whatever meat you had and squeeze for a few seconds. It's funny I pinch my youngest son the same way. The rule is when you can't pop, pinch. It taught me that there would be consequences for my actions.

The most impactful coach came in my junior year in high school. His name is Charles Brady. To say that he was just a head football coach would be a disservice. Leader, philosopher, developer of boys to men would be more fitting. He cared about winning the game of life more than winning on the field. He saw football as a vehicle or platform to help prepare us for life. God placed him in my path to mold and shape my character. We all were treated as his own. I felt obligated every game and every play to leave everything I had on the field to make him proud.

It was our homecoming my senior year. We were playing our coaches' former team. There was some bad blood between the two so this game was very important to Coach Brady. This was the time to make him proud with a W so I thought. It was my first game playing running back. I ran for 118 yards on 11 carries with 2 touchdowns and 1 interception. That was not enough to win the game.

I remember one of the plays that potentially lost the game for us. It was option left, the quarterback pitched the ball behind me and they recovered the fumble inside our 20-yard line. At the time of the fumble I was at the bottom of the crowd holding on the ball. I totally blanked out to the point where I heard no whistle, teammates, or refs. It took all of them to pry the ball away from me. I didn't let go because I didn't want to let coach down. I cried that night. I left it all on the field.

Are you doing the same for God? How do you reward your mentor or people who invest in you? God invested and sacrificed everything, even his only Son. How do you honor him? Being a true disciple of Christ honors God. From this day forward acknowledge and nurture everything and everyone God has put in your life.

Action point: Prayerfully choose a Mentor who will instruct you in wisdom and understanding ... and help you avoid some potholes on your journey.

Step 5

Forgive Forward

Col 3:13

Make allowance for each other's faults, and forgive anyone who offends you. Remember, the Lord forgave you, so you must forgive others.

How do you like to travel? Light or heavy? Do you pack a weeks' worth of clothes for a weekend getaway? Are you still packing the morning of your flight? It may sound silly but so many of us walk around every day with extra baggage. That baggage gets heavy and overwhelming overtime. That same baggage stops the flow of new life and hardens the heart. Sometimes we don't even realize that we are carrying all this dead weight. What am I talking about? Unforgiveness.

It is tearing you apart from the inside out. Let's together stop the bleeding and begin to repair and restore this wound of unforgiveness. Some of your blessing are being blocked because of it. The bible states in Matt. 5:*23* *"If you are offering your gift at the altar and there remember that your brother has something against you, leave your gift there in front of the altar. First go and be reconciled to your brother; then come and offer your gift".*

Forgiving someone is one of the most liberating feelings that you will ever experience. Somewhere down the line, forgiveness was looked at as a weakness. Oh, how wrong we were. Forgiveness is for us not them. Being able to forgive is a major strength. After all we have also received forgiveness from sin that we could never have paid for, so we must forgive.

Jesus paid the price for our sins. John 3:16 states *"For God loved the world so much that he gave his one and only Son, so that everyone who believes in him will not perish but have eternal life".* I shared my story during Phase 1 about how I held in so much anger towards my father to the extent that it almost destroyed me. Now I will allow my sister to tell hers:

"My dad always threatened to kill my mom if she left him. My mom finally got the courage to leave my dad. We went to my grandmother's house so we could be with my granddad for protection. We had to go to school the next morning, therefore; my granddad took us home to get some clothes for school. As we pulled in the driveway at our house, I saw someone look out the window. I told my mom and granddad, but they thought I was just scared and seeing things. We entered the house and when we got in, my mom could tell someone had been there. She said, "He's been here, let me call the police." My dad came running out of the bathroom with a gun screaming, "Don't you dare call the police!" I was standing right at the door, but was too frightened to open it. My sister reached over me and opened the door. We ran out. My sister and I were holding hands. As we were separating, it seemed as though I could feel the wind of the bullet go between us. Yes, my dad was shooting at us! My granddad and my dad got into a shoot-out. My dad grabbed one of my brothers as a hostage. My brother was scraped on the leg by a bullet while being held hostage. My dad had escaped before the police could come to our rescue. This is just one of the incidents that caused me to have sleepless nights because of nightmares. This is one of the incidents that caused me to be scared to walk into an empty house. This is just one incidents that caused me to turn on every light in the house and search every room before getting comfortable. This is just one of the incidents that caused me to fear my dad.

Forgiveness is essential for happiness and personal growth. For years, I walked around with the burden of unforgiveness. It was a heavy load on me that I didn't realize was so heavy until I finally forgave. I always wondered what was stopping my blessing because I am a person who always try to find a way to bless others. I have always been a jolly person with a great personality, but something was missing and altering my complete happiness and growth. Finally, it hit me! It had to be the voice of God speaking to me about forgiving my father.

I could forgive anyone else easily, but not my father. My father had taken me and my family through so much pain, fear, and agony. The day I finally decided I was going to forgive my dad, I planned to visit him in prison the next visiting day. I had always loved and cared for him, but I was just so angry and afraid of him. I cried all the way to the prison. I could already feel the weight on my shoulders getting lighter. When I made it to the prison my dad was shocked to see me. It had been years since I had spoken to or seen him. He reached out to hug me and I hugged him back. We cried on each other's shoulder. I looked my dad in the eyes, with tears running down my face, and a runny nose and said, "Dad I forgive you." My dad apologized to me for all the pain he had caused. After I released my unforgiving spirit and fear toward my dad, my darkness was turned to light, my shoulders were light as feathers, my mind was at peace as though a 2-ton weight had just been rolled off, and God began to shower blessing on me like never before. I began to see that God was my bridge over troubled water. I didn't believe this before because all I was thinking was there isn't a God, because he wouldn't have let my family go through all we went through. Now I know there is a God and He is Alive! We are not supposed to be here or even in our right minds with everything we saw, experienced and lived as children. All our trials, challenges, tribulations were just a set- up for our step up! They didn't break us, they only made us stronger."

Your story may not be as traumatic as this but any unforgiveness big or small has the same affect. Maybe someone wronged you in the past. It could have been your mother, father, sibling or friend and you have yet to release that negative seed of unforgiveness. I will let you in on a secret. Suppressing pass hurt does not put you in the clear. You will have to deal with that pain at some point or you will end up being the person hurting someone else. Hurt people hurt others. Do yourself a favor and find a way to mend any broken relationships that exist in your life. Not only to help you move forward with your life but to be obedient to the word of God.

He commands us to reconcile with one another. As you can see through his word God is very serious about how important relationships are. He loves us all and hates anything that separates us from Him. I have a mechanism that will help end the cycle of hurt in your life. I call it RR&R. Reflect, Release, and Renew. Reflect on your past pain and hurt. Pray to God and ask him to cleanse your heart of any resentment that you may be holding against anyone. Next Release it to God. It's not your battle to fight. Cast your cares on Him. He will give you peace. The final step is to renew your mind. Replace thoughts of pain with thoughts of peace, comfort and joy which comes from the Lord.

Action point: say dear Lord, I release everyone I'm holding up in my heart and I allow your love to take me over while I fulfill your purpose in this life in Jesus

Step 6

Get involved with helping others

Luke 6:38

"Give, and you will receive. Your gift will return to you in full—pressed down, shaken together to make room for more, running over, and poured into your lap. The amount you give will determine the amount you get back."

We were created to serve a purpose. Let me break that down for you with an emphasis on the word serve. Per the dictionary, serves means to perform duties or services for another person or an organization. That means that you were created for something bigger than yourself. I will put this where the goats can get it. Your life is not about you; so, get over it. The sooner you can grasp the concept, the sooner your life will become significant.

For me, serving others to help them reach their full potentials has, and always will be more important than money.

Do you wonder at times how people have a perfect job with great benefits and great pay and they still seem miserable? It's more common than you think. Part of the reason is that either conscious or unconscious, people want their lives to count. They want to matter and make a difference but their job limits their potential impact.

Most people coast under the radar and continue to accept being marginalized. Slowly, but surely it starts to pick at your confidence and you find yourself in a very bad place. There is now a void that needs filling and guest what? There is a void in society that only you can fill. Will you have the courage to answer the call? Someone's life out there depends on you being what God created you to be. God already preordained it. You are not waiting on Him. He's waiting on you to move.

I am the baby boy of 6 kids. There are 4 boys and two girls. Every summer we could not wait to go swimming. I didn't know how to swim so I asked my brother to teach me. He agreed. Once we got to the pool he took me to the deepest end. I started having second thoughts before I could back out my brothers picked me up and threw me in…. You better believe that I learned how to swim by trying to survive in the water. If it was up to me, I may had waited to the "perfect time". Are you waiting for the "perfect time" to get involved with helping others? Stay with me now. A couple years later, I was able to save someone from drowning. What if I never learned how to swim?

Albert Einstein once said, "The world is a dangerous place, not because of those who do evil, but because of those who look on and do nothing." Jesus was a servant leader that ultimately laid down his life for us. In John 15:12-13, it reads "This is my commandment: Love each other in the same way I have loved you. There is no greater love than to lay down one's life for one's friend." God loves and rewards a cheerful giver. So, give yourself to others without expecting anything in return. Share generously and devote yourself to uplifting others. When you pour into to others, others will pour into you. You get what you give.

Zig Ziglar said "You can have everything you want in life if you will just help enough people get what they want." One thing that really upsets me is when people in leadership roles are under the misconception that people are in place to serve them when it should be the other way around. I've experienced this far too many times in my career. Most of my "leaders" taught me how not to treat people. It's amazing though how the world will blackball you for doing what is right. I speak from experience. Trust me on this. I was one of the few leaders that would stand up and fight for the people I served regardless of whether it was against my supervisor or the president of the company.

If you have the responsibility of leading others, it's your duty to protect and develop them. When you have a passion for Christ and doing what is right, being passive is not an option. One of your main purposes in life is to help produce and develop disciples for the body of Christ. Always remember the "Golden Rule." Do unto others as you would have them do unto you. You will need help throughout your journey so make time to fellowship with Believers.

Action point: Stop seeing life as being all about yourself. Help others to fulfil their dreams and you will be fulfilling yours in doing so.

Conclusion

We have been able to consider some major points as we get transformed in our lives and our ministries. We have seen that it is very expedient to have mentors on the road to being a success. It is God's divine idea that men should help other men on their journey into destiny. God didn't create man to self-exist.

The life of Joshua was useful to God only when he learnt so much from Moses. When Moses died, God had no problem in looking for a replacement. Joshua was thoroughly prepared already for the task. Little wonder God didn't start to give him new teachings, he simply instructed him to follow everything Moses had laid down which he had also learnt.

Having a mentor in life will avail us the opportunity of not making the same mistakes that people ahead have. Instead of learning by experience, we simply learn by instruction. Moses lacked a Mentor and He took him forty more years to be ready for the use of God but it was not so with Joshua.

In the same breath, we looked at developing your "WHY". Setting your motive and priority right. Having an unmovable foundation. It is so important because it will avail you benefit of unwavering focus. Without a well-developed why, everywhere will look like your destination. You need to have a solid ground as the reason behind your actions

Lastly, having and keeping a winning attitude is not negotiable if you are success driven. Any other person can afford to sell on credit but not you. You can't be complacent about life and success will fall on your laps. You need to be deliberate about life, you need to be deliberate about chasing God who alone placed greatness inside of you. Don't just be an accident happening all around.

Leave the camp of men that don't have a mentor, leave the camp of men who don't have a ground and basis, leave the camp of men who are complacent. Join the camp of men that chase after God and are deliberate about being a success in life.

The Journey To Better

10 Steps of Transforming Poverty into Prosperity

The Transformation Series:

Phase 3- The Growth Process

Introduction

Before poverty can be transformed into prosperity, there are certain principles of life that must be strictly adhered to. Breaking them is staying at the back side of the wilderness. For example, we considered keeping a winning attitude in the preceding series. Keeping a winning attitude is one principle that will always transform poverty into prosperity.

Scripture says as a man thinking in his heart so he is. You can never amount to something important in life if you can't envision yourself that way first. Bible says in 3rd John vs. 2, *Dear friend, I hope all is well with you and that you are as healthy in body as you are strong in spirit.* I want you to take note of the last sentence. It says even as thy soul prosper. That simply means the prosperity of the physical is predicated upon the prosperity of the mind.

It will take a prosperous mind to prosper physically. However, to prosper in our minds, we will consider certain steps that will guide our transformation process. For example, our emotions, how we feel about something is also a component of our mind. In the same vein, we will consider growth as factor in our transformation process. Someone cannot grow beyond his mindset because it will either boost or limit his desires for growth.

There is no man born of woman that will love to start out miserable in life but quite a few people are. What then can be responsible for that? I discovered that the access into the right knowledge per time makes a difference in people's lives. No wonder Paul was praying for believers to know, to come into undertaking of their advantages in the kingdom. It is important we know and that is the reason you have this book in your hands. To bring you into the right knowledge you need per time to make a good success of your life and purpose in God.

Step 7

Master your Emotions

Rom 8:35

"Who shall separate us from the love of Christ? shall tribulation, or distress, or persecution, or famine, or nakedness, or peril, or sword?"

The next step in your journey will lead to a lasting legacy. Winning is one thing but building a legacy is another. Think of the Alabama Crimson Tide football program, the New England Patriots, Duke or Kentucky basketball. What do they all have in common? They are dynasties. Love them or hate them you can't refute the truth. People lie but numbers don't. Rome wasn't built in a day neither were these programs. It took hard work, long hours, discipline, and endless sacrifices for everyone involved. The same opportunity exists for you if you are willing to give up to go up to the next level. Are you ready to learn how?

Imagine you have not learnt how to master your emotions through God's word, when distress or tribulations comes, you will be tempted to let go of your aspirations in God.

That is why Apostle Paul said what shall separate us from the love of God? He went ahead to list a couple of things which largely anchor on our emotions.

Your emotions hold the key to your success. How you feel about yourself determines what you see. Emotions are like double-edged swords. They can determine success or failure. They make us happy or sad. They sometimes cloud our judgment. They sometimes lighten the load. Sometimes they weigh heavy on our hearts. But however, emotions are necessary. God created us as emotional beings. Fear is an emotion. Worry is an emotion. Even though neither is of God. How you may ask? I will go ahead and nip that in the bud quickly.

If God is the head and in control of your life, what need is there to worry or fret? The real problem arises when E.G.O. steps in. E.G.O. means Edging God Out. We want to be in control and toss it to God when things spiral out of control. When you operate without control, you operate outside of the grace of God. Therefore, we must learn to manage our emotions rather than allowing them to manage us.

On another note to be honest, without emotions this world would be a very boring place. Just think about that for second. How a movie would be without emotions, better yet a wedding if no one cried tears of joy. The important thing about emotions is the inspiration it gives us to move into action.

I will like to help you start up with the right actions by aligning yourself with the word of God. Not the action when you go into Wal-Mart for one thing and come out with a basket full. Your emotions made you feel like you needed and had to have all the extra stuff. You went over budget and now you are running late. Plus, you still need to get what you came for in the first place. Does that sound like any of you? That's on a lighter note. Making decisions based solely off your emotions can make you lose your job, marriage, and in some cases your life. Acting off emotions reveals cracks in your character and leave a gaping hole for the devil to enter through the flesh. We were born of flesh and blood which makes us vulnerable from outside attacks. Whatever you feed into your system via Radio, TV, etc. will determine your emotional response.

Our emotions should be grounded in truth. The truth is the word and the word is God. Every time we ingest negativity, it withdraws from our soul account. On the other hand, all positive things deposit seeds for a future harvest. That's why it's important to stay in the word. Staying in the word and meditating renews your mind and allows you to have the mind of Christ. Just like a computer system, every now and then you must reboot. Your CPU will get backed up and start to slow down making your system vulnerable to viruses. CPU stands for Christian Processing Unit. When this is damaged, you mind is not protected.

Some people think that going to church on Sunday alone will keep them filled throughout the week. That's rather funny. The same as a car with a V8 engine by Wednesday morning they are running off fumes. Then again it might be Monday morning if it is regular gas (word of God) and not premium. So, make sure that you are attending a bible based church. Like I said before, this is mental and spiritual warfare. The helmet of salvation is the most important weapon in your possession to defeat the enemy. This will take discipline. Good intentions will not secure a victory. Start living a life of intentionality. Change your mind set from trying to doing.

#Do not base your life on your feelings#

If you are looking for the definition of instability, study emotions, then you will understand instability. In other words, one of the most unstable things you can ever find on the surface of the earth is emotions. If you will wait till you feel like doing, then you may never do the necessary at the necessary time. To do the necessary at the necessary time is one of the keys to achieving anything at the time expected. You will find a very elated person crying a few seconds after laughing over a very funny matter. Times and again, you may find yourself feeling like not doing anything, please, your decision to work should not be based on feelings.

> **Action point:** Refuse to allow what you feel to blur your vision. Paul said what shall separate   us from the love of God? No point of emotion can, be it distress or discouragement.

Step 8:

Develop Your Why

Luke 14:28-30

"But don't begin until you count the cost. For who would begin construction of a building without first calculating the cost to see if there is enough money to finish it? Otherwise, you might complete only the foundation before running out of money, and then everyone would laugh at you. They would say, 'There's the person who started that building and couldn't afford to finish it!"

At this point the building blocks are in place and there will be nothing but smooth sailing from here. Right? Absolutely not, the journey is just beginning. The good news however is that you are in position for a breakthrough if you persevere and stand on the word of God through all the trials and tribulations that life will throw at you. It will not be comfortable nor convenient to hold the teaching of our Lord. Therefor we must protect our minds with the helmet of salvation.

Let me slow down a little before I get ahead of myself. It will be nearly impossible to embrace or encompass any teaching without a strong "Why" to fuel your desire to succeed. If you cannot have a strong reason why you are doing what you are doing or why you want to do it, you might fizzle out after a little while.

For a case study, let's examine Demas from the scriptures, when he was following Paul. They got to Thessalonian and he forsook Paul. It means he had a very wrong priority from the beginning. He was overtaken by the lust that is in the world.

Why was Paul able to scale through against all odds? Paul had defined and developed his why. He had stated that in the face of persecution, rejection, peril, poverty and even death, he would stay true to the course of Christ. As a matter of fact, he went through almost everything he had aforementioned. Yet, he was able to stay strong and courageous. He defined his Why and founded it on a solid rock so much that when persecution and peril arose, he stood still and unmovable.

Without a strong "Why", you might be tempted to quit on your life's pursuit when you face a real storm or adversity in life.

From a biblical standpoint, I strive to be a better person and to be who God created me to be. Why? You may ask. I want people to see God in me. I believe that my job as a believer is to glorify God in every aspect of my life, after all we are made in His image. I understand that everyone is a work in progress and not all are on the same level. Don't get discouraged by comparing your walk with others.

Before I received the "Good News" of the living God, my main motivation or "Why" revolved around making my mother proud and providing hope to my immediate family. This reason fueled me to be better and do better to positively impact future generations. Every time I think of my "Why" the hair on my neck rises, I catch chills and emotions run high. At times, it's hard to stop crying. The same burden that was put on me by my mom at the age of 16 still carries the same if not more weight as time passes. I can never do enough to payback all she has sacrificed for me and my siblings.

If your "Why" doesn't make you cry you will only put just enough effort or just enough sacrifice to get by. If this is the case for you, take some time to search deep from within. First ask yourself the following questions: What am I deeply passionate about? What wakes me up in the morning? What burns in me like fire? What is my purpose in life? What do I want people to say about me at my funeral? Answer these questions sincerely and your truths will be revealed. Seek and you shall find.

Your why is so important because it provides meaning to the mission. We all ultimately desire to be significant whether we are willing to admit it or not. The why unlocks the supernatural power that exists within us? It's the same power that resurrected Christ from the dead. Speaking of Jesus Christ and a why, In Romans 4:25, it states that He was handed over to die because of our sins, and he was raised to life to make us right with God. Now does that help put things in perspective for you? Your why will never be about just you. If you think so, you are delusional about reaching your full potential. The FBI calls that a clue. There is a saying "Where there is a will, there is way." But I say, "where there is no why there is no way."

You see, the why is what the mitochondria is to the living cell. It's the powerhouse. It's where the magic happens that gives you the will and drive to succeed. It's hard to stay the course if you are counting on your will alone to get you through. One guarantee is that your will power will soon run out. To combat this, your words and actions must be aligned with your why. So, take the time to be in the right mind. Do this by spending time with the master and meditating on His word.

Action point: Consider your "Why" whenever you feel discouraged or ready to give up.

Step 9

Adopt a Winning Attitude

1 Cor. 9:24-26

"Don't you realize that in a race everyone runs, but only one person gets the prize? So, run to win! All athletes are disciplined in their training. They do it to win a prize that will fade away but we do it for an eternal prize. So, I run with purpose in every step. I am not just shadow boxing."

This is one scripture that helps in refocusing our priorities. It helps us to align our minds to the true course which we started out to follow. So many people are in the race of life for varied reasons. Some because of others, some because of pressure some because of their parent's expectations.

Paul here nailed it all. He stated emphatically that the only ones that will win in life are the ones that keep a winning attitude. He said, "so run that ye may win". Many are running not because they want to win. It is expedient that you know why you are running. Are you in the mixed multitude for the fun of it or you want to really make a difference by winning?

If winning is your priority, then being temperate in all things will be your core aim. What does it mean to be temperate? It means to keep a winning attitude, to shun every form of distractions whether it be luxury or suffering.

It is said that winners don't quit and quitters don't win. In other words, persistence and determination are core attitudes of winners. Have you ever wondered what separates the winners from losers? What is the secret to success or failure? What is the special sauce that all winners possess that is contagious and help raise others to higher levels? Some might say the number of W's in the win column. If you ever played sports you've probably heard or seen this quote. "Winning isn't everything, it's the only thing."

The #1 ingredient in my opinion to success is a positive attitude. Your attitude will always be the difference maker. It is the factor that enables people to transition from good to great. Unfortunately, some of us are forced into negative environments where we allow life to beat us down and destroy all hope for a better future. This environment then shapes your reality and it's hard to think positive when you are surrounded by negativity. Now in your eyes, you see lose-lose situations which sets up for a life of mediocrity and that's not in God's plan for your life.

You win or lose before you enter the ring. Even in a defeat there is never a failure, only lessons to prepare you for greater opportunities. Sometimes you will win other times you will learn. Never take a loss empty handed. Leave with something that will add value to your experience. We all have setbacks but we don't all handle them the same. Some get discouraged and give up. These are the ones that throw a pity party and complain about everything. Those same ones will do nothing to change their situation. They play the blame game and they love to attempt to contaminate your positive stream of life.

There is no faith involved in their daily decisions and they threaten your Christian walk. I say threaten because these are some of your close friends or relatives. Take a moment and analyze your circle of friends and family. Do they fit the description? If so, stand clear of them because they can be standing between you and your relationship with God. There is no judgment or condemning involved, you just need to detach before you are derailed. Your loyalty will be questioned so be prepared.

On the other hand, there are those who see challenges as opportunities to grow. They live outside of the boundaries set by man and exercise their faith daily. They don't complain but rather remain grounded in the word of God. They are the overachievers. The world might call them sell outs. I've been called that amongst other things. Like "stop acting white or acting like you are better than us."

Those comments come about when your progress makes people uncomfortable in their own skin. It's not your fault but it was your choice to change the game. Everyone has that same choice. So be unapologetic for your growth and success. Take time to pray for the lost and intercede on their behalf. They may want to hold you back but they need to see you succeed. You may be that one example they needed to break free.

At times, you will be the only God that people see so allow the Holy Spirit to lead and guide you. The only difference between these two types of people is attitude. Which one are you? The choice is yours to make so make the right one. You can't go wrong with Jesus steering the wheel. Every child of God has victory through Christ Jesus.

You must also bear in mind that it is a part of a positive attitude never to quit even when everything seems to be pointing in that direction. Abraham Lincoln failed 999 times, but in the long run, he won. Ben Carson, the world-renowned neuro-surgeon was once labelled a dullard, however, he never quitted being a student; today, he is a celebrated surgeon. The same applies to you. You might have tried everything within your powers to leave that position of yours; to leave from poverty to wealth and affluence, yet all to no avail, bear in mind that if you do not grow weary, you will win.

#Renew your mind#

Someone once said, "What you believe, you will receive". It is quite unfortunate that many a people are living with a poverty mentality. It's pertinent to renew one's mind, if one would really transform from the kingdom of poverty to that of prosperity. Whatever is too big for your heart and mind to conceive, is too big for you to receive. In other words, if you don't change your thought pattern, from "I can't" to "I can", you will remain where you are, irrespective of the number of principles you adopt.

Action points: Develop a mental toughness that will help your preserver through life challenges. Always remember that God is the source for all victories.

Step 10.

Focus on Growth

1 Peter 2:2

"As newborn babes, desire the sincere milk of the word that ye may grow thereby"

Growth is the most crucial factor in Christian living. It is absolutely necessary and compulsory for growth to take place. The same way a child needs to grow when given birth to, also spiritual children need to go up into the fullness of Christ.

According to Gal 4 vs. 1, you cannot be given to handle even though you are a child unless you grow. The very reason is because you will make a shipwreck of whatever is given you unless you grow up.

One of my mentors and business associate John C. Maxwell states that "Change is inevitable. Growth is optional." I agree with this statement whole heartedly because growing involves stepping outside of your comfort zone. Most people chose convenience or comfort over their true calling.

Growth is optional because it takes a daily decision to be committed to something greater than yourself. People that chose comfortable lives are like a reservoir or the Dead Sea. There is no flow of new life. There are no expectations. They are very content with just existing. God can't use this type of person. Guest what? The church is full of them. They religiously attend all church functions and can quote the word like no other yet they do nothing to advance the Kingdom.

In some cases, they detour people from having a relationship with God because of judgment and condemnation. God doesn't give brownie points for you soaking up knowledge from the tree of life for yourself. He equips you with it to spread the Gospel and develop more believers. A good tree produces good fruit. So, what are you producing if anything? Jesus talks about this type of person with regards to the second coming. Matthew 7 NLT verse 21-23 states "Not everyone who calls out to me, "Lord! Lord!' will enter the Kingdom of Heaven. Only those who do the will of my Father in heaven will enter.

On judgment day, many will say to me, 'Lord! Lord!' We prophesied in your name and cast out demons in your name and performed many miracles in your name.' But I will reply, 'I never knew you. Get away from me, you who break God's laws.' The other type of person choses to live on purpose. They seek out God's instructions. They invest time not only in studying the word but applying what they learned in their daily lives to advance the Kingdom. These are the true disciples that keep His commandments and bear much fruit.

The difference in the two are vast. One is stagnant while the other flourishes. Matthew 7:24-27 states "Anyone who listens to my teaching and follows it is wise, like a person who builds a house on solid rock. Though the rain comes in torrents and floodwaters rise and the winds beat against that house, it won't collapse because it's built on bedrock. But anyone who hears my teaching and doesn't obey it is foolish, like a person who builds a house on sand. When the rains and floods come and the winds beat against that house, it will collapse with a mighty crash." I have a question. Which one are you? You don't have to answer that right now but know this if you are serious about reaching your full potential, growth must be a top priority and it is not negotiable.

The closer you grow up to the measure of the fullness of Christ, the more you develop the mind of Christ. The more you meditate on his teaching, the closer you get to know your purpose. When you figure out your purpose growth will become intentional not an option. You are not born into the person you become. That's why you must purposely grow into who God created you to be.

Action points: Consciously take responsibility for your growth. Have a workable plan of study, meditation and be intentional about your growth. Set S.M.A.R.T. goals for yourself every day.

Conclusion

It is with boundless joy that I welcome you to the conclusive end of this series. I believe it has greatly transformed your life. Without transformation, there can never be manifestation. Quite a lot of people are wandering about in the world, bitter against God, bitter against themselves and others around them.

To journey successfully in this world and to also fulfil out God given dreams and purpose, we must walk according to the pattern in the manual. The manual which is God's word has outlived every manual that has ever existed, the source is eternal and it is the only manual that can bring about an eternal transformation in our lives.

Every other manual is of the earth but this is the living manual that gives purpose to the purposeless, hope to the hopeless, joy to the broken hearted, and life for the lifeless. The more we see ourselves in the mirror of God's word, the more we are changed into the same image we behold from glory to glory. If we can strictly follow the plan of God for our lives, we will discover that the sky is the beginning of unlimited resources.

It is not enough to have read this masterpiece written by the help of the Holy Spirit, the most important thing is to put every detail to heart and make a practice of them. Do not just get excited about the great truth you have read from this series but be a doer. I promise, if you follow the steps provided in this series you will be able to transform your life and relationships to help you reach your full potential.

Let's Get Connected

Please connect with me via social media:

https://www.linkedin.com/in/wallacegabriel

twitter.com/journey2better

gabrielgwallace.com

www.facebook.com/gabe.wallace.779#

https://www.facebook.com/growthovertime